POPULAR
SONGS
HAL LEONARD
STUDENT PIANO LIBRARY

Tchaikovsky's
The Nutcracker Suite
Six Easy Arrangements for Piano Solo

Arranged by Lynda Lybeck-Robinson

T0081622

ISBN 978-1-4950-2799-4

HAL•LEONARD®
CORPORATION
7777 W. BLUEMOUND RD. P.O. BOX 13819 MILWAUKEE, WI 53213

In Australia Contact:
Hal Leonard Australia Pty. Ltd.
4 Lentara Court
Cheltenham, Victoria, 3192 Australia
Email: ausadmin@halleonard.com.au

Visit Hal Leonard Online at
www.halleonard.com

CONTENTS

Arabian Dance
("Coffee")

By Pyotr Il'yich Tchaikovsky
Arranged by Lynda Lybeck-Robinson

Moderato (♩ = 96)

Chinese Dance
("Tea")

By Pyotr Il'yich Tchaikovsky
Arranged by Lynda Lybeck-Robinson

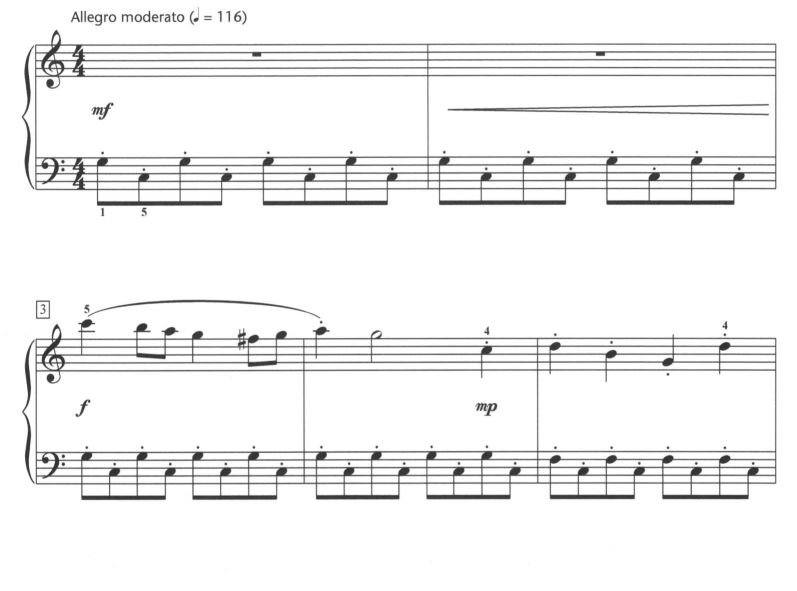

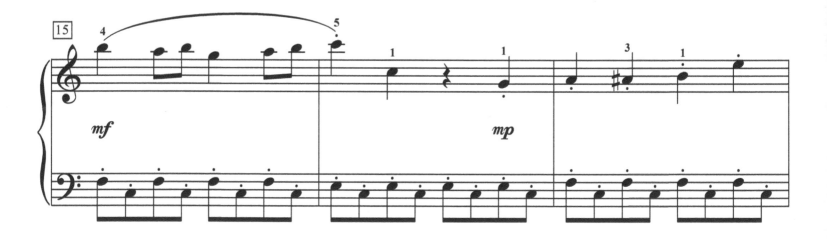

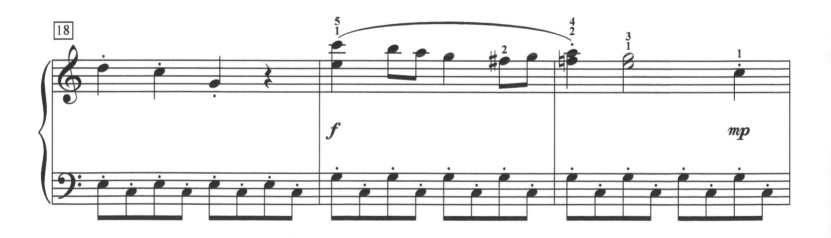

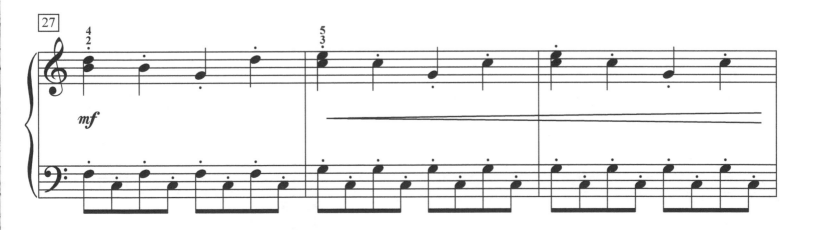

Dance of the Sugar Plum Fairy

By Pyotr Il'yich Tchaikovsky
Arranged by Lynda Lybeck-Robinson

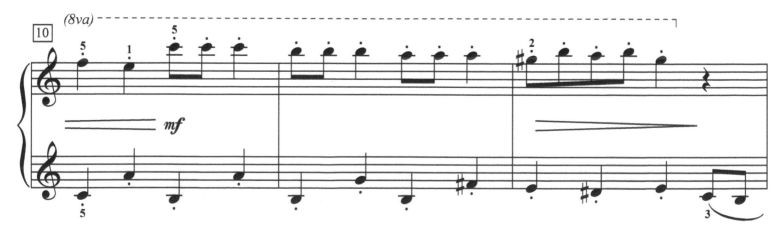

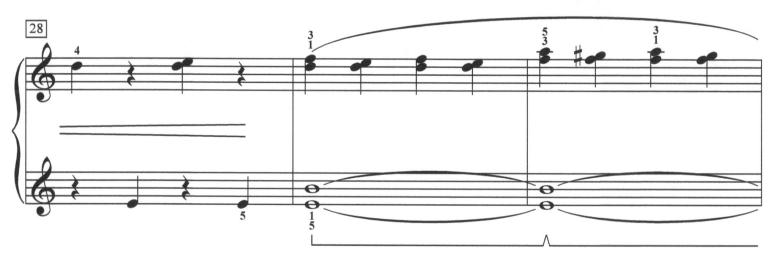

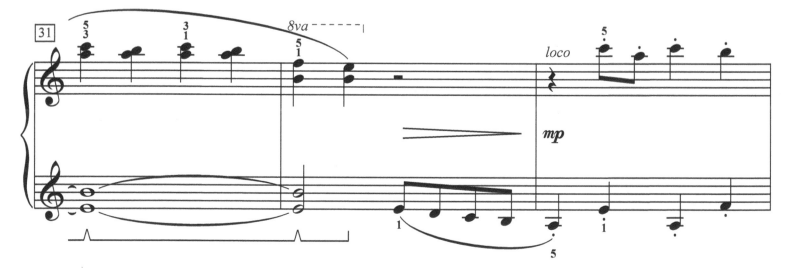

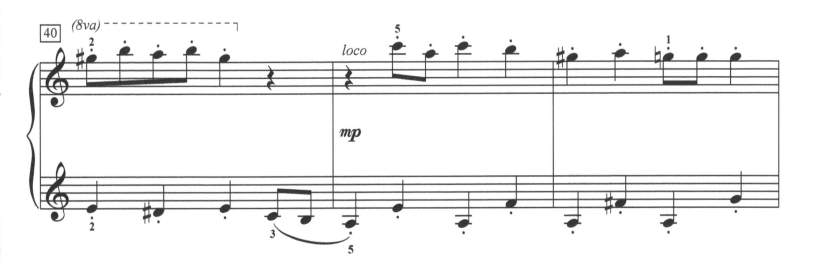

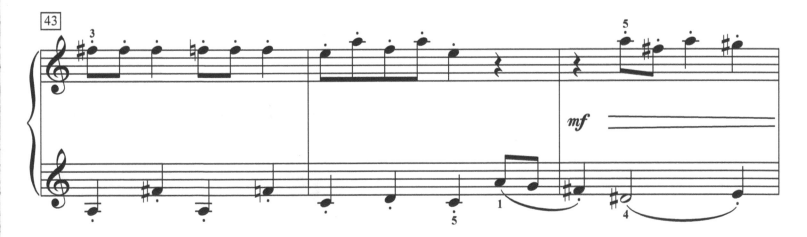

March

By Pyotr Il'yich Tchaikovsky
Arranged by Lynda Lybeck-Robinson

Moderato (♩ = 132)

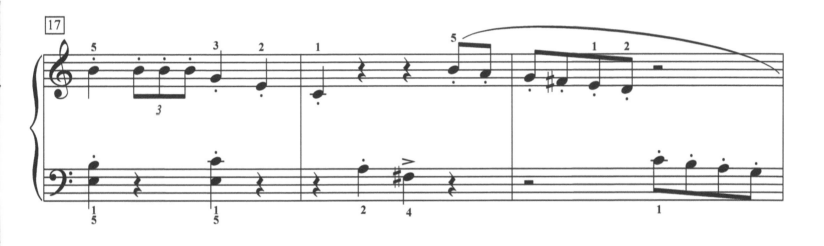

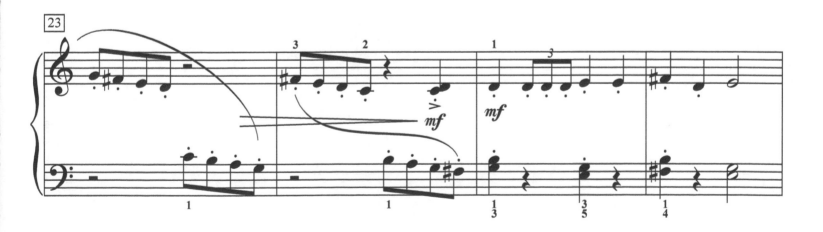

Waltz of the Flowers

By Pyotr Il'yich Tchaikovsky
Arranged by Lynda Lybeck-Robinson

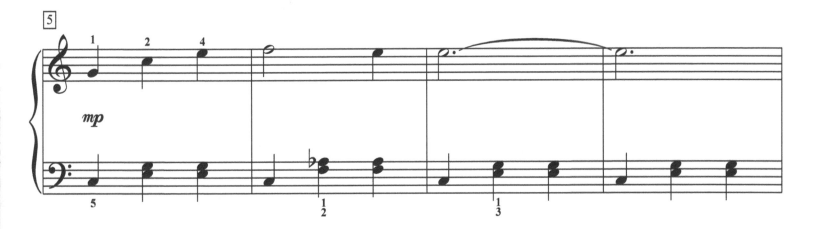

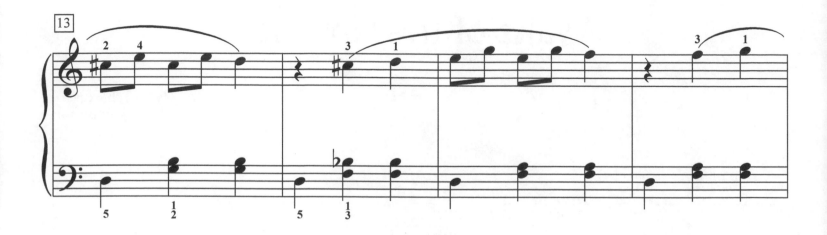

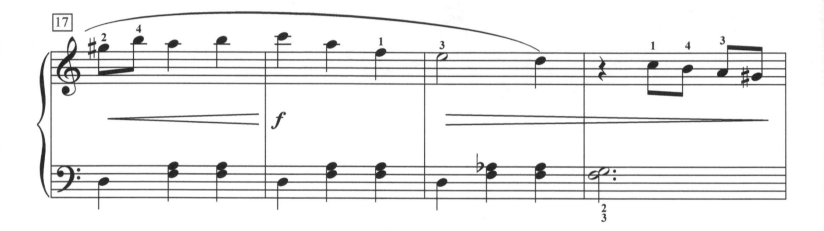

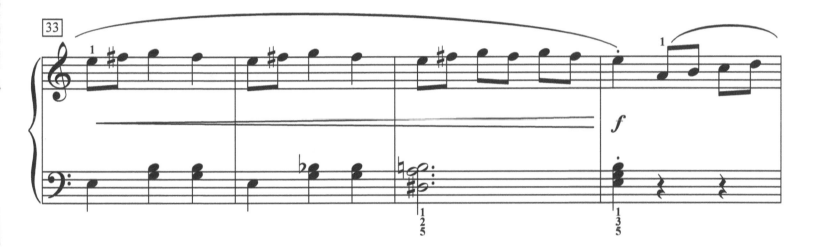

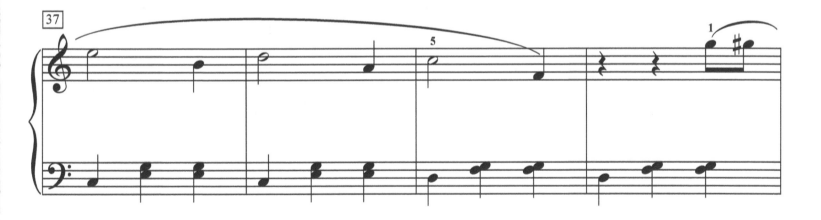

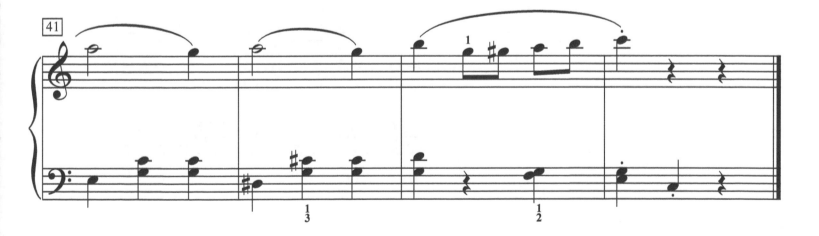

Russian Dance
("Trepak")

By Pyotr Il'yich Tchaikovsky
Arranged by Lynda Lybeck-Robinson

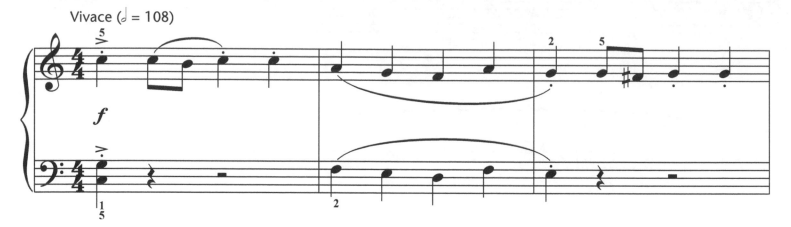

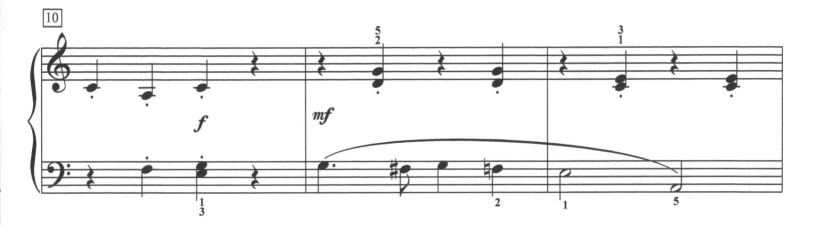

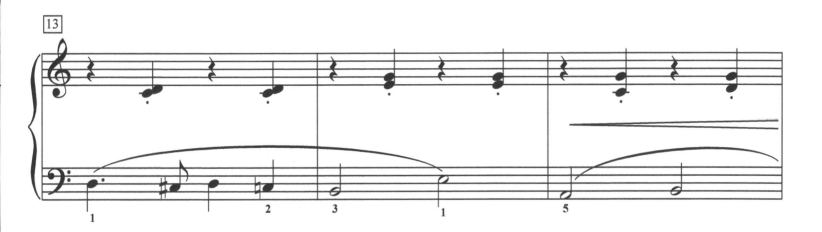

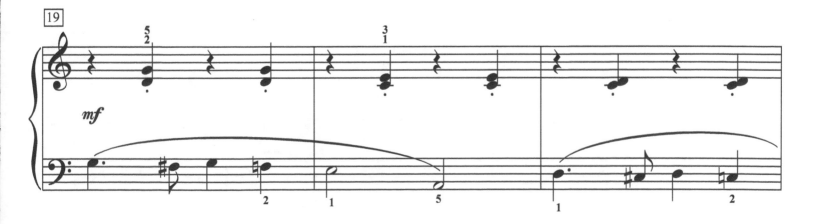

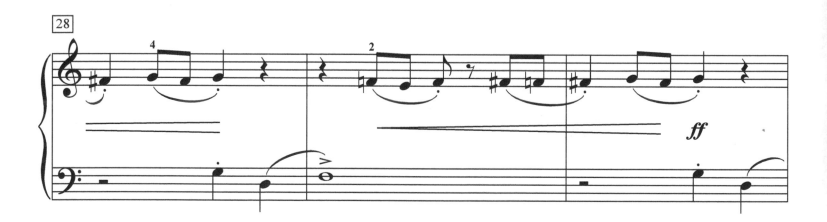

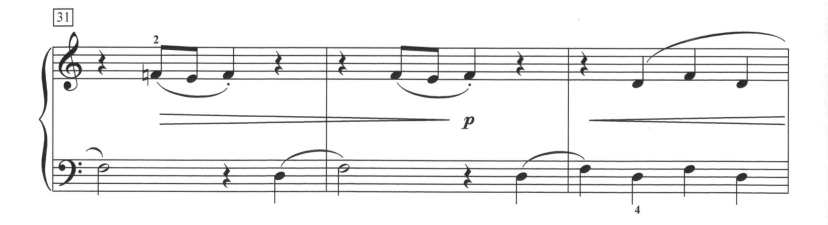

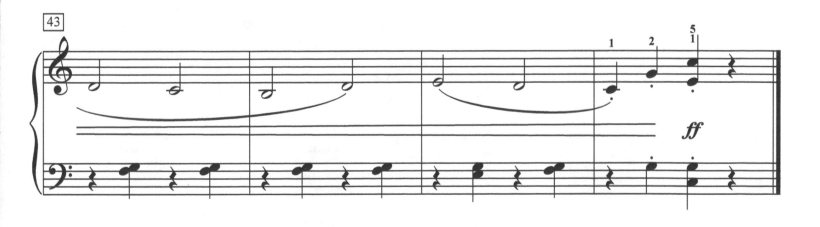

POPULAR SONGS
HAL LEONARD STUDENT PIANO LIBRARY

The **Hal Leonard Student Piano Library** has great songs, and you will find all your favorites here: Disney classics, Broadway and movie favorites, and today's top hits. These graded collections are skillfully and imaginatively arranged for students and pianists at every level, from elementary solos with teacher accompaniments to sophisticated piano solos for the advancing pianist.

Adele
arr. Mona Rejino
Correlates with HLSPL Level 5
00159590...............................$12.99

The Beatles
arr. Eugénie Rocherolle
Correlates with HLSPL Level 5
00296649...............................$12.99

Irving Berlin Piano Duos
arr. Don Heitler and Jim Lyke
Correlates with HLSPL Level 5
00296838...............................$14.99

Broadway Favorites
arr. Phillip Keveren
Correlates with HLSPL Level 4
00279192...............................$12.99

Chart Hits
arr. Mona Rejino
Correlates with HLSPL Level 5
00296710...............................$8.99

Christmas at the Piano
arr. Lynda Lybeck-Robinson
Correlates with HLSPL Level 4
00298194...............................$12.99

Christmas Cheer
arr. Phillip Keveren
Correlates with HLSPL Level 4
00296616...............................$8.99

Classic Christmas Favorites
arr. Jennifer & Mike Watts
Correlates with HLSPL Level 5
00129582...............................$9.99

Christmas Time Is Here
arr. Eugénie Rocherolle
Correlates with HLSPL Level 5
00296614...............................$8.99

Classic Joplin Rags
arr. Fred Kern
Correlates with HLSPL Level 5
00296743...............................$9.99

Classical Pop – Lady Gaga Fugue & Other Pop Hits
arr. Giovanni Dettori
Correlates with HLSPL Level 5
00296921...............................$12.99

Contemporary Movie Hits
arr. by Carol Klose, Jennifer Linn and Wendy Stevens
Correlates with HLSPL Level 5
00296780...............................$8.99

Contemporary Pop Hits
arr. Wendy Stevens
Correlates with HLSPL Level 3
00296836...............................$8.99

Cool Pop
arr. Mona Rejino
Correlates with HLSPL Level 5
00360103...............................$12.99

Country Favorites
arr. Mona Rejino
Correlates with HLSPL Level 5
00296861...............................$9.99

Disney Favorites
arr. Phillip Keveren
Correlates with HLSPL Levels 3/4
00296647...............................$10.99

Disney Film Favorites
arr. Mona Rejino
Correlates with HLSPL Level 5
00296809 ....$10.99

Disney Piano Duets
arr. Jennifer & Mike Watts
Correlates with HLSPL Level 5
00113759...............................$13.99

Double Agent! Piano Duets
arr. Jeremy Siskind
Correlates with HLSPL Level 5
00121595...............................$12.99

Easy Christmas Duets
arr. Mona Rejino & Phillip Keveren
Correlates with HLSPL Levels 3/4
00237139...............................$9.99

Easy Disney Duets
arr. Jennifer and Mike Watts
Correlates with HLSPL Level 4
00243727...............................$12.99

Four Hands on Broadway
arr. Fred Kern
Correlates with HLSPL Level 5
00146177...............................$12.99

Frozen Piano Duets
arr. Mona Rejino
Correlates with HLSPL Levels 3/4
00144294...............................$12.99

Hip-Hop for Piano Solo
arr. Logan Evan Thomas
Correlates with HLSPL Level 5
00360950...............................$12.99

Jazz Hits for Piano Duet
arr. Jeremy Siskind
Correlates with HLSPL Level 5
00143248...............................$12.99

Elton John
arr. Carol Klose
Correlates with HLSPL Level 5
00296721...............................$10.99

Joplin Ragtime Duets
arr. Fred Kern
Correlates with HLSPL Level 5
00296771...............................$8.99

Movie Blockbusters
arr. Mona Rejino
Correlates with HLSPL Level 5
00232850...............................$10.99

The Nutcracker Suite
arr. Lynda Lybeck-Robinson
Correlates with HLSPL Levels 3/4
00147906...............................$8.99

Pop Hits for Piano Duet
arr. Jeremy Siskind
Correlates with HLSPL Level 5
00224734...............................$12.99

Sing to the King
arr. Phillip Keveren
Correlates with HLSPL Level 5
00296808...............................$8.99

Smash Hits
arr. Mona Rejino
Correlates with HLSPL Level 5
00284841...............................$10.99

Spooky Halloween Tunes
arr. Fred Kern
Correlates with HLSPL Levels 3/4
00121550...............................$9.99

Today's Hits
arr. Mona Rejino
Correlates with HLSPL Level 5
00296646...............................$9.99

Top Hits
arr. Jennifer and Mike Watts
Correlates with HLSPL Level 5
00296894...............................$10.99

Top Piano Ballads
arr. Jennifer Watts
Correlates with HLSPL Level 5
00197926...............................$10.99

Video Game Hits
arr. Mona Rejino
Correlates with HLSPL Level 4
00300310...............................$12.99

You Raise Me Up
arr. Deborah Brady
Correlates with HLSPL Level 2/3
00296576...............................$7.95

HAL•LEONARD®
7777 W. Bluemound Rd. P.O. Box 13819 Milwaukee, WI 53213

Prices, contents and availability subject to change without notice. Prices may vary outside the U.S.

Visit our website at www.halleonard.com

0321
009